NEATH & PORT TALBOT

Snapshots

NEATH & PORT TALBOT
Snapshots

By David Roberts

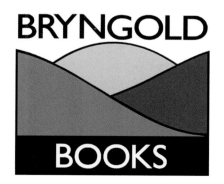

BRYNGOLD
BOOKS

First published in Great Britain in 2007 by
Bryngold Books Ltd.,
Golden Oaks, 98 Brynau Wood, Cimla,
Neath, South Wales, SA11 3YQ.
www.bryngoldbooks.com

Typesetting, layout, editing
and design
by Bryngold Books

ISBN 978-1-905900-02-2

Printed and bound
in Wales by
Gomer Press
Llandysul, Ceredigion.

Contents

Appreciation

THE fascinating collection of remarkable images of the past in **Neath & Port Talbot Snapshots** shows the willingness and enthusiasm of a growing number of people to share their photographs and to play a part in recording the social history of both towns.

Some have contributed just a single picture, others many more. Each one however, is as important as the next in a book that can not only be enjoyed by today's readers, but will also serve as a record for future generations.

Particular appreciation for their involvement is due to: Cheryl Roberts, my wife, without whose support none of these books would have appeared; Anthony Isaac, the late Vincent Thomas, John & Barbara Southard, the late Eric Hill, Colin Scott, John Vivian Hughes, David Slee, Robert Thomas, Mike Hoile, Keith & Ann Davies, the late Ken Kingdom, Lynsey Sly, Allun Davies, Elaine Wise, Wyndham & Julie Griffiths, Roger & Veronica Gale, Betty & Mervyn Roberts, Annette Jones, Neath Port Talbot Library Service; Alwyn Rees, Anita Thomas, Audrey Walters, Betty Hall, Bernard Humphries, Colin Walters, David Jones, Debbie Lines, Debbie Shawe, Geoffrey Nicholas, Jeff Thomas, John Howells, John Matthews, John Newman, Kay Maclean, Marlene Webb, Mr & Mrs D Williams, Ron Williams, Mrs Eileen Cottey, Janice Austin, Mrs V Gardener, Mrs Val Thomas, Norman Reed, Paul Davies, Val & Mike Davies, Peter Sodestrom, Peter Stephens, Robert Alan Jenkins, Steve Dinham, Steve Williams and Andrew Pearson for his assistance with the cover design.

Pictures please!

IF you would like to contribute photographs to the next Neath & Port Talbot book — **a special 10th anniversary edition** — and play a valuable part in this growing pictorial archive please telephone 01639 643961 or e-mail bryngold@btinternet.com. All photographs — black and white or colour — of people, places, events, schooldays and sport — are considered whatever their age, subject or format. They are all promptly returned. Also, if you have missed any of the previous books why not contact us now. We would be delighted to hear from you.

Foreword

HAVING collected all the previous editions of David Roberts' excellent books it is a great thrill to provide the foreword for this latest volume.

Neath and Port Talbot Snapshots is a unique photographic record of the people and places of our towns and indeed our lives. Much more than that, it reflects the changing social scene of our own particular part of the world.

Every edition of this wonderful series of books is a cross generational bridge, where parents and grandparents sit down with their families to reminisce on times past. We laugh at the changing fashions and wonder at the different social trends. Everybody marvels at the far reaching structural changes that have occurred over the passage of time.

I myself savour the atmosphere and memories that every picture evokes. They say a picture is worth a thousand words — if that is the case then these volumes say a great deal about our lives and the communities in which we live.

I wish David well with **Neath & Port Talbot Snapshots** and look forward to seeing the 'new' old photos that bring memories of all our yesteryears flooding back.

**Councillor
Anthony Taylor,
Mayor of
Neath Port Talbot
County Borough
2007-08**

New for old

THE word 'new' has heralded many changes throughout the towns of Neath and Port Talbot in recent times. The arrival of new homes, shops, commercial enterprises, roads and even the people they often bring with them, have all played a part in what has become an almost seamless metamorphosis.

Many will consider this a healthy sign. It is, after all, a demonstration that the two towns are keeping pace with the fast-moving 21st Century. Others will lament the fact that often, to make way for this newness, much of what went before has to be swept aside. Their views are an indication of the conflict that is bound to exist as our towns continually reshape themselves to meet modern demands. Both sides are, of course, right in their thinking and their sentiment.

Change in itself is not new, however. Neath and Port Talbot differ in so many ways but are united in their desire to remain vibrant and prosperous. This has been the case from their earliest beginnings. That has always meant change is unavoidable and inevitable.

Much that we have experienced down many decades is mirrored in the images of **Neath & Port Talbot Snapshots**. The title is apt because most of these pictorial peeps at the past are just that – snapshots in time encapsulated forever.

Added together these fascinating photographs will unite generations and maybe even spark a yearning to discover exactly what all this newness has replaced. In a way they will also reveal some of the very foundations of the towns we know and hold dear today.

Switch on the TV, turn the pages of any local newspaper and what is happening right here, right now, will be evident. Turn the pages of this book and what will be revealed is much of what has paved the way for these developments in the never ending story that is Neath and Port Talbot.

**David Roberts,
2007**

Changing Places

The tower of St Thomas parish church stands sentinel over The Square, Neath, 1954. For many years Phillips Bros was one of the town's larger retail outlets.

Looking westward along High Street, Aberavon, early 1900s. The canopied River Afan bridge dominates the centre of this scene today.

A young girl poses for the cameraman amid lines of drying clothes and a tin bath hanging on the railings in the narrow alleyway that was Zoar Row, Neath, 1952

A typical scene in Water Street, Port Talbot, with the town's municipal buildings under construction in the background, along with the main Paddington to Swansea railway bridge, 1912.

Traffic heads out of Neath along Bridge Street past the old riverside leather warehouse, mid-1950s. The scaffolding was erected around the building prior to its demolition.

Part of the site of the former cattle market at Neath, which closed in 1958 ready for the retail development which followed. The general market building alongside survives to this day.

One of the residents of Mansel Street, Port Talbot, outside her home, early 1920s.

Two youngsters take a break on the bridge that led to Neath's old Fairfield, 1949.

The Big Parade was the main attraction at the Palace Cinema, Water Street, Aberavon, when this scene was captured in 1920.

Empty animal pens at the old cattle market, Neath, 1958. It was relocated shortly after to make way for retail development. The Market Tavern can be seen on the right.

Traffic waits at the level crossing at High Street, Port Talbot, for a goods train to pass in April, 1948. Closure of the gates regularly caused long road traffic delays. Plans for a town by-pass were being discussed at this time, but it was 1966 before the motorway was opened.

A fascinating aerial view of Aberavon town centre 1949. St Mary's Church can be seen with the town's former general market to its right. Mountain Junior School is visible at the top.

The Parade, Neath, at its junction with Green Street, 1965.

High Street was the main A48 east-west traffic route through Port Talbot and not often as quiet as when this mid-1960s picture was taken. The library occupied the former TT Lloyd's store.

The Gnoll Cinema, Gnoll Park Road, with the Gnoll School alongside, February 1959. A tyre depot and divisional police headquarters respectively have now replaced them.

A unique view of Maes yr Haf chapel through the structural steelwork of new retail units being erected in front of it on Windsor Road, Neath, early 1960s.

Looking down on High Street, Aberavon, mid-1960s.

Construction work underway on the
M4 Pentyla flyover at Port Talbot,
June, 1963.

A Ford Consul saloon was the attraction in the Alfred Street, Neath, showroom of CEM Day, in 1959. Building of a new Briton Ferry & Neath Co-operative Society store can be seen on the right.

A very busy High Street road bridge over the River Afan, Port Talbot, 1960.

Church Street, Aberavon, showing the Crown Hotel on the right, mid-1960s. In the distance is High Street, once the main east-west traffic route through the town.

The retail units built in The Parade, Neath, on the site of the town's former cattle market, shortly before completion, 1960. Construction of further units can be seen on the right.

The Municipal Buildings and shopping arcade, Aberavon, shortly before they were demolished, 1972. One of the town's two FW Woolworth stores can be seen on the right.

Contractors move on to the Bird in Hand Field, Neath, to begin construction of the town's former Civic Centre, early 1960s.

Looking towards Gnoll Avenue, Neath, through the ornate Gnoll Lodge Gates, 1964.

Construction work on the elevated section of the M4 motorway at Port Talbot, 1964.

Building work in progress on Neath Civic Centre, 1964. St David's Church can still be seen through the concrete structural work. The building has now been replaced and is scheduled for demolition.

The railway level crossing gates at High Street, Port Talbot, that caused so many traffic delays on the A48 trunk road until the opening of the new M4 motorway, 1966.

The Globe Hotel, High Street, Aberavon, looking towards the River Afan road bridge, 1967.

Boarded up shops in Water Street, Aberavon, await demolition to make way for town centre redevelopment, 1971.

Neath railway station forecourt, March 9, 1969.

Albert Terrace, Aberavon, during its demolition to make way for town centre redevelopment during the late 1960s.

The garage of Llew Evans & Son which stood at the junction of London Road and Creswell Road, Neath, 1965. The site was formerly home to Neath's tramway depot.

Three names familiar to shoppers on Green Street, Neath, are clearly visible, though the Maypole grocery store had relocated shortly before this 1966 photograph was taken.

High Street, Aberavon, showing demolition in preparation for town centre redevelopment, late 1960s. The Mountain School overlooks the scene.

Neath Rural District Council offices, Orchard Street, Neath, 1966. The properties alongside were later demolished to make way for expansion of the town's Woolworth store.

The Ivorites Hall, at the junction of Richard Street and Church Street, Port Talbot, 1969.

Talbot Square, Aberavon, showing the Post Office, 1970. The area was swallowed up by town centre redevelopment.

The popular Phillips department store, New Street, Neath, 1966 when it was still a busy traffic thoroughfare. The town's Civic Week was underway at the time.

A slice of life from the sky. This unusual aerial portrait of Port Talbot, was taken in 1975 and shows clearly the influence of road, rail and river on the town.

Crown Buildings, sandwiched between the Angel Hotel, left, and Neath's old Town Hall, 1967. Demolition of the building had already started.

Forge Road, Port Talbot, early 1980s.

The Midland Bank and some of the other commercial premises that drew shoppers to Station Road, Port Talbot, late 1960s.

Orchard Street, Neath, on November 10, 1968, showing the start of demolition of the former Neath Rural District Council offices to make way for an extension to the town's Woolworth's store. The town's Constitutional Club with its impressive architecture can be seen on the right.

Looking eastwards along Station Road, Port Talbot, 1979.

Prefabricated homes, or prefabs as they were known, at Gnoll Bank, Neath, 1968.

Workmen remove slates from the roofs of houses in lower Water Street, Port Talbot, shortly before their demolition, 1985.

While some interesting advertising hoarding characters look down on him, Howell Gwyn's statue looks down on passers-by outside the Gwyn Hall, Neath, 1968. The statue now stands within the gates of nearby Victoria Gardens. His birthplace was opposite and today a plaque on the wall of the town's Woolworth's store indicates this.

An atmospheric view of Victoria Gardens bus station, Neath, after an overnight snowfall, February 1969. St David's Church is in the background.

Looking down on the Talbot Athletic Ground, home to Aberavon RFC, with part of Port Talbot and its docks in the background, 1985.

Frayne the Saddler's house, High Street, Neath, before demolition in December 1972. An Iceland frozen food store is here now.

The Plaza Cinema, Talbot Road, Port Talbot, late 1980s. Though it is boarded up now, in its heyday it showed plenty of big screen hits.

The former vicarage of St Theodore's Church, latterly Port Talbot Arts Centre, Port Talbot, 1985.

The lane between Connaught Street and George Street, Port Talbot, looking towards Abbey Road, December, 1985.

Looking down Windsor Road, Neath, towards Stockham's Corner and the town's Methodist Church, 1972

Looking westwards along Station Road, Port Talbot, shortly before pedestrianisation, late 1980s.

A view eastwards along Windsor Road, Neath, 1972.

A view across the roundabout at Stockham's Corner, Neath, towards Eastland Road, 1975.

The Halfpenny Bridge across the River Afan at Port Talbot, 1987.

Looking over the rooftops of Neath town centre from Cook Rees Avenue, 1983.

Ysguthan Road, viewed looking towards Port Talbot town centre, June 1987.

There was an eyecatching brickwork logo at this car sales site in Water Street, Port Talbot, October, 1987. A hotel and restaurant now stands on this site.

Houses at the eastern end of London Road, Neath, near Stockham's Corner roundabout, 1971.

Pedestrianisation work underway along Station Road, Port Talbot, June 1987.

London Road, Neath, looking towards the town's Victoria Gardens, early 1970s.

Early steel erection work underway as part of the Neath town retail development, 1988. Today this is the site of the car park for Morrison's supermarket.

Talbot Road, Port Talbot, with the Eagle Street junction on the left and the town's Royal British Legion Club on the right, late 1970s.

The Gnoll Primary School, Gnoll Park Road, Neath, August 1989.

Port Talbot Magistrates Courts alongside the town's main railway station, August 23, 2002.

Men and machines combine their efforts to secure the demolition of the Gnoll Primary School, Gnoll Park Road, Neath, May 1993.

Groundworks in progress on the site of the Castle Surgery, Prince of Wales Drive, Neath, formerly Foner's scrapyard, alongside the Neath Canal, February 11, 1990.

The last days of Fletcher's car showroom, Gnoll Park Road, Neath, May 1993. Work is already underway to turn the building into a tyre and exhaust service centre, 1993.

Neath Police Station, Windsor Road, February 1990. It became the David Prothero pub and restaurant after a new police headquarters was built at Gnoll Park Road on the site of the Gnoll School.

Familiar Faces

Women and girls from Abergwynfi in the Afan Valley sold postcards to raise funds to support the men from the village who were away fighting in the First World War, 1914-18.

Sunday school teachers, deacons and officials of the Wesleyan Methodist Church, London Road, Neath, 1930.

Members of the sisterhood at Bethlehem Chapel, Aberavon, 1933.

Patients and nursing staff at Cimla hospital, Neath, February 27, 1948.

Regulars at the Star Inn, Penydre, Neath, with the pub's landlady, Mrs Smith, early 1950s.

Taking a welcome break from their labours are these volunteers who undertook the task of building Goytre Community Centre, Port Talbot, 1950.

Mr & Mrs Pulman, of Elias Street, Neath, with their 12 children, gathered together for a family celebration, late 1940s.

Regulars of the Star Inn, Penydre, Neath, mid-1960s.

Officers of Neath Girls Guildery make a presentation to Mrs Burridge, the wife of the minister at Neath Methodist Church, when the couple left for a new posting, 1953.

Officers and committee members of the British Legion's Port Talbot and Aberavon Branch, mid-1950s.

Some of those who attended the annual fancy dress party organised by Neath Amateur Operatic Society, mid-1950s.

A group of young women friends at Goytre Community Centre, Port Talbot, 1955.

The Jersey Arms, Cwmavon, was the venue for the reception of this wedding group who lined up outside the building when this one for the album was taken, late 1950s.

A group of women employees from the Metal Box factory, Neath, at a retirement function held to say farewell to one of their colleagues, early 1960s.

Staff and friends of the Vivian Hotel, Aberavon, at the nearby Antolin's Ros-a-Mar Rooms during a farewell celebration for landlady Mrs Selina Jones, on her retirement, 1963.

A special Old Time Musical Hall night provided the excuse for these members of Val Snow's Keep Fit Class to dress up. Apart from enjoying themselves their efforts also cheered up some of the patients at Neath Hospital Annexe. The event took place in the Wellfield Hall, 1966.

Singer Allun Davies meets staff of Red Dragon Relays, Eaglesbush House, Neath, to thank them for their support during his successful run on TV's Opportunity Knocks programme, 1965.

Members of a popular Port Talbot keep fit class, 1964.

Mayor of Neath, Councillor R. Lloyd Davies, with members and officials of Neath and District Schools' football squad when they visited the mayor's parlour at the town's civic centre, 1968.

Members and officers of Taibach Workingmen's Club after the opening of a new extension at the Dyffryn Road premises, 1966.

Fancy dress was the order of the day for these members of a charity group run by employees of Freeman's cigar factory, Port Talbot, seen while distributing gifts to the needy, Christmas 1980.

The silver wedding celebration of Harold and Alice Oates was the reason for this family gathering at Antolin's Ros-a-Mar Rooms, Victoria Road, Aberavon, 1968.

Members of the board of governors of Dyffryn Comprehensive School, Port Talbot, June 1982.

Members and officers of the Skewen division of the St John Ambulance Brigade after a presentation evening, 1979.

The staff of Colour Care photo processing laboratory, Neath Abbey Industrial Estate, hand over a charity cheque for the Children in Need appeal at their Christmas celebration, 1986.

Entertainer Frankie Vaughan OBE seen during a visit to Port Talbot to officially open the Margam Youth Activities and Leisure Centre on Friday, September 3, 1982. Behind Frankie is Clive Thomas, Welsh International referee and president of the Welsh Boys' Clubs organisation.

A group of residents of the Gnoll Nursing Home, Gnoll Park Road, Neath, gather in front of the building to watch a passing parade, 1988.

When Councillor Olga Jones became Mayor of Port Talbot she invited a group of her former school chums from Margam to pay a visit to the Mayor's parlour, 1983.

Out of Town

Housing alongside Neath canal at Giant's Grave, Briton Ferry, early 1900s.

The imposing, main flower-bed flanked walkway of Vivian Park, Sandfields, Port Talbot, with its bandstand behind, 1958.

Two pictorial panoramas of summertime days at Aberavon Beach. The one above showing the Jersey Beach Hotel captures the mood around 1909, while left, crowds throng the sands and promenade in the late 1920s.

Dyffryn Mansion, Bryncoch, Neath, plays host to a garden fete, early 1900s.

New Road, Skewen, was not such a busy thoroughfare when this 1915 scene was captured.

The grand facade of the Public Hall at Briton Ferry, 1920.

Two Port Talbot footbridges each serving a different purpose. One spanned the River Afan at Corlannau, the other the railway to Cymmer, recently removed when this 1967 picture was taken.

The reservoir on the Earl of Jersey's estate at Briton Ferry, mid-1920s.

Little traffic moved on Margam Road, Port Talbot, one of the town's main thoroughfares, after heavy snowfall, February, 1978.

Neath Abbey Road, Neath, looking towards Skewen, 1935.

Neath Abbey Road, Neath, looking towards town, 1935. CEM Day's garage and car sales site is now on the right about here.

The view up Bwlch Road, Cimla, towards Crynallt House, early 1900s. A close look reveals two figures at the top of the lane. The house remains to this day, but the greenery around has long since been swallowed up by housing.

The attractive hamlet of Groes, Margam, 1975. Soon after it vanished under the ongoing march of the M4 motorway.

Film fans head into the Lodge Cinema, Briton Ferry, shortly after it opened in 1937.

The 230ft high cooling towers of BP's Llandarcy oil refinery seen through the trees in Cook Rees Avenue, Neath, April 1968.

The main shopping parade at Commercial Road, Taibach, early 1970s.

A view across Cwmavon showing St Michael's Church and Tabernacle Chapel, mid-1970s.

The picturesque second pond at the Gnoll Park, Neath, 1983.

A view of the entrance to Port Talbot docks at the mouth of the River Afan, 1975.

Traffic heads over Beach Hill bridge, Aberavon, towards the seafront, June 1987. The bridge, originally built to carry traffic over the Rhondda & Swansea Bay Railway line was removed in 2006.

Building of sheltered accommodation on the site of the former Lodge Cinema and bingo hall at Briton Ferry, late 1980s.

The Esso petrol filling station at Aberdulais, on the former A465 Swansea to Birmingham trunk road, April 26 1994. The Dulais Rock pub is on the upper right hand side.

Some of the excavators and heavy earth moving machinery employed in the removal of coal deposits from a sunken vessel at Aberavon Beach, late-1970s.

The residents of Glynclydach House, Longford, Neath Abbey, enjoy a summer's afternoon on the lawn, early 1900s.

Vehicles almost buried by deep snow at Avondale Terrace, Cymmer, Port Talbot, during 1982.

The view towards Port Talbot from the M4 motorway's Neath river bridge taken during a charity walk along it, shortly before it was officially opened on February 26, 1993.

Restoration work underway with the aid of heavy machinery on the promenade at Aberavon Beach, after severe erosion by heavy seas, 1997.

The dualling of the nine mile long Aberdulais-Glynneath stretch of the A465 at a cost of £45.7m began on January 10, 1994 and opened to traffic on February 24, 1997. This giant gravel pit provided foundation material and was later flooded to become a large lake alongside the road.

Construction of the A465 Neath Valley dual carriageway at Ynysygerwn, 1995. The clubhouse of Ynysygerwn Cricket Club can be seen at the top of the embankment.

Young Ones

Stepping up for the cameraman – literally – is this smartly dressed group of young Goytre, Port Talbot, boys, early 1950s.

Two Neath children pose with their pet dog, 1918.

Three young smartly-dressed Sandfields children in the garden of their home, early 1950s.

Some of the members of Neath Boys Club, mid-1920s.

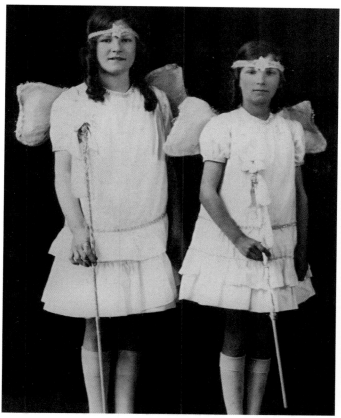

Two Neath sisters dressed for their parts in a play at Herbert Road School, Neath, 1920s.

Young Sandfields girls dressed to celebrate the Coronation of Queen Elizabeth II, June, 1953.

Bill Higgins with his horse who was a popular attraction for the children of the Court Herbert House estate, Neath, early 1930s.

Cousins and friends of Martyn Jones, Cimla Crescent, Neath, share an interest in his new Raleigh tricycle, early 1950s.

Three Port Talbot children wrapped up in their winter coats enjoy a chilly trip to the park, 1953.

Youngsters ready for action with their bows and arrows on Smith's Hill, Goytre, Port Talbot, 1950s.

Members and officers of the Cilfrew group of the St John Ambulance Brigade, outside their meeting hall at Penscynor, Neath, late 1930s.

A gathering of Goytre, Port Talbot, children, 1958.

William Thomas — known as Will Bwt — at his home, 24 Union Road, now Penydre, Neath, with two granddaughters, 1939.

Members of Cadoxton Youth Club, Neath, at their annual concert, late 1940s.

A group of energetic youngsters ready to pedal off on their bikes at Goytre Road, Goytre,
Port Talbot, 1959.

Arm in arm in friendship, two young girls at Taibach, Port Talbot, 1952.

Holding hands in Union Road, Neath, now Penydre, 1951, needed a little persuasion!

A pupil of Herbert Road School, Melyncrythan, Neath, with a Welsh doll for a chum on St David's Day 1958.

Two young boys take a break from their playtime exploits in the garden of their home at Handel Avenue, Sandfields, 1966.

Building a snowman on Margam Road, Port Talbot, after the heavy snowfall of February 1978.

Neath Guides with their leader during an annual camp at Saundersfoot, Pembrokeshire, 1959.

Some of the lads who were members of Grange Street Church Boys Club, Port Talbot, with its leader, Mr Vivian Evans, 1978.

Youngsters all dressed in their Sunday best stand at The Parade, Neath, and watch the passing Whitsun procession of the town's churches, 1955.

Participants in a pantomime production of Snow White and the Seven Dwarves held at Bethesda Chapel, Sunday School, Hoo Street, Briton Ferry, early 1950s.

Members of the 1st Baglan Guide Troop on a day trip, 1985.

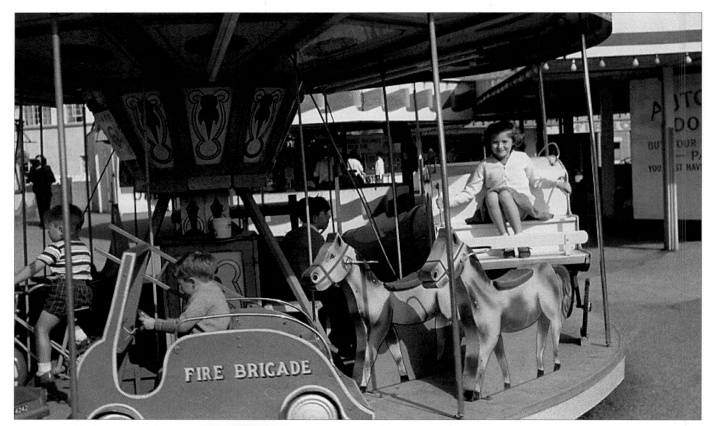

A children's roundabout was just one of the attractions at the Miami Beach Funfair, Aberavon, August 1965.

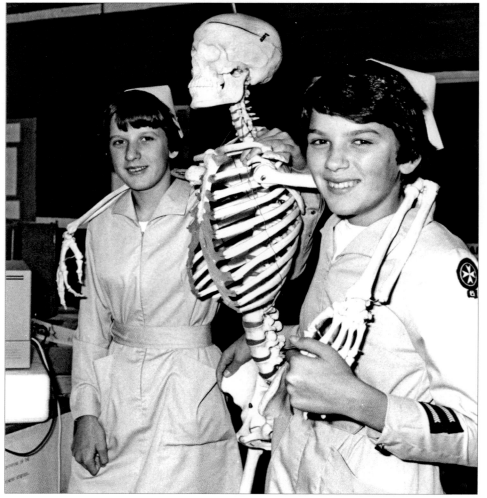

Sisters Helen and Andrea Morris, members of the Skewen division of St John Ambulance Brigade with a practice skeleton, during a Festival of Youth at the Afan Lido, Aberavon Beach, November 19, 1983.

Shopping Spree

There was no mistaking the fact that JH Taylor's, Neath Road, Briton Ferry, was a butcher's shop as this early 1900s picture shows.

This group is standing outside a shop in Queen Street, Pontrhydyfen, 1910, owned then by Megan Lewis and later Evan Williams. Latterly it was the recently-closed Pontrhydyfen sub post office.

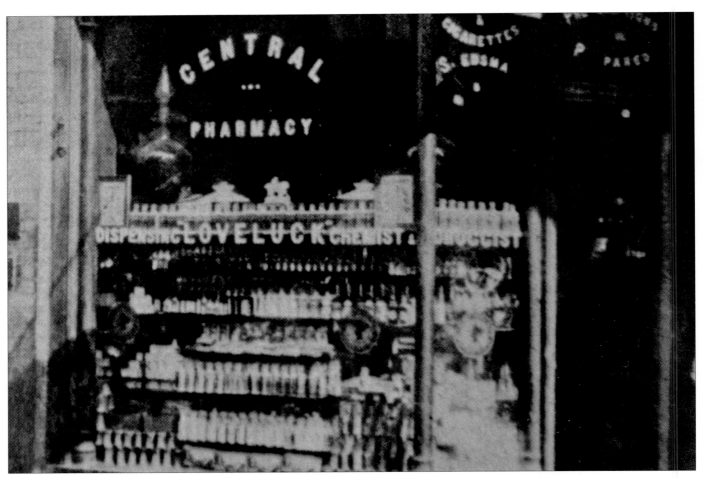

The general pharmacy run by GD Loveluck, Water Street, Aberavon, early 1900s. The store stocked everything from abdominal belts to surgical appliances.

Standing proudly outside their store are the staff of Peglers grocery store, High Street — now Commercial Road — Taibach, early 1920s.

Stan Pope and his wife behind the counter of their Pandy Stores at Morgan's Terrace, Pontrhydyfen, 1932.

The Windsor Road, Neath store of T Griffiths, florists and fruiterers, early 1900s. Mrs Griffiths can be seen holding her son Ven, with a shop assistant alongside.

Chidzoys green-grocery store was to the right of this amazing picture. It shows the queue that formed when word leaked that they had received a consignment of fruit shortly before Christmas in wartime 1944. The queue can be seen snaking from the front of the store around the back of the Majestic Cinema, later the Odeon and out into the street again. Aberavon Town station is on the left of an area now occupied by the town's Tesco store.

The Wholesale Tobacconist store, at No. 6 New Street, Neath, 1910.

Four of the women who served behind the counter of Peglers grocery store, Taibach, 1948.

SALE! SALE! SALE!

JOHN LEWIS & SON

'Star Shop,' Villiers Street, Briton Ferry,

beg to announce that their GREAT WINTER SALE will

Commence on FRIDAY next,

when £5,000 worth of Men's and Boy's Clothing, Hosiery, Blankets, and
Drapery will be offered at ridiculously low prices to ensure a Speedy Clearance.

Here are just a few of the Bargains we are offering you.   Come early and get the pick.

Men's Suits—Latest Styles, Smart Patterns—29/11.   Honestly worth 49/11.

Boys' Suits—Strong for School Wear—from 6/11.   A Plum.

Men's Overcoats and Raincoats from 29/11.   Latest Styles.   Usual Price 49/11.

Boys' Overcoats from 4/11, to clear.   Ridiculously Cheap.

Men's Trousers 4/11½.   Youths' Long Trousers 3/11½   Strongly made.

Boys' Knickers 1/11¾.   Worth Double.

Men's Shirts 2/11½, to clear.   Job Lot.   Good Quality.

Men's and Women's Stockings from 6¾d.   Worth Double.

Men's Pants and Vests 1/11¾.   Wonderfully Cheap.

Boys' Fancy Top Stockings 1/6¾.   Any Sizes.   All Wool.

Blankets—Full Size—2/11¾—Worth 4/11.

And many other Bargains too numerous to mention.

☞ SEE WINDOWS!   SEE WINDOWS!! ☜

TAILORING.—Our Tailoring Department is still going strong.   We are making
all the Latest Styles in Suits and Overcoats.   Give us a Trial, you will be
delighted.   Money back if not perfectly satisfied.   Style and Fit Guaranteed.

Mourning Orders executed in 12 hours

Don't forget the Address—

JOHN LEWIS & SON,

"STAR CLOTHIERS," Villiers St., Briton Ferry.

It seems there was plenty to attract the bargain hunting shopper when the Star Clothiers store of
John Lewis & Son at Villiers Street, Briton Ferry held a sale in 1910.

Staff at the Wind Street, Neath, store of
Boots the Chemist, 1957.

The Maypole grocery store and Red
Lion pub, at the junction of Water Street
and High Street, Aberavon, during town
centre demolition 1972.

Handbags and trolleys were the order of the day for these shoppers in Station Road, Port Talbot, on a chilly spring day in 1980.

Some of the staff of the Taibach and Port Talbot Co-operative Society store at Commercial Road, Taibach, 1948.

Stallholder Arthur Cole with his assistant Arthur Roberts at the Neath Market butchery stall of EC Cole, mid-1930s.

Graham Rees, a stallholder at Neath General Market, 1988.

Shops around the Odeon Cinema, Bethany Square, Port Talbot, prior to demolition early 1980s. It was home to bingo rather than films at the time and had reverted to its original Majestic title.

Proprietors Mr & Mrs Eric Hill in the doorway of Hills Cycle Shop, Windsor Road, Neath, late 1970s. This was their second premises in the road. The first, nearer Stockham's Corner was demolished during construction of the town's Southern link road.

Stan the Cobbler's shop, 14 London Road, Neath, September 1978.

Sid and Colin Rees on the last day of trading at the popular fruiterers store they ran next to the Workingmen's Club, Wind Street, Neath, July 29, 1989.

All the latest domestic appliances of the time were on view for customers at the Wales Gas showrooms at Victoria Road, Aberavon, mid-1970s.

Learning Curve

A class of girls with their teacher at Sandfields Junior School for girls, 1920.

A group of infant pupils at Briton Ferry National School, 1911.

Pupils of class 2A at Sandfields Council School, Port Talbot, 1923.

Forms 3 and 4 at Alderman Davies' Girls' School, Neath, 1929.

Pupils of one of the classes at Briton Ferry Board School for girls, 1924.

Form 3C at Neath Boys Grammar School, 1946.

A class at Eastern Infants School, Taibach, Port Talbot, 1925.

Girls of Gnoll Primary School, Neath, with American exchange teacher Alice Jewel from Arizona, July 18, 1951.

Pupils and teachers from Port Talbot Secondary School before setting off on a trip to the Rhine in Germany, Easter 1938. The cost of their trip was about £8.50.

Pupils of Tywyn Primary School, Sandfields, with their teacher and headteacher, 1953.

A group of pupils from Gnoll School, Neath with their teacher at Ogmore Youth Camp, 1951.

Pupils of Eastern Infants School, Port Talbot, during celebrations to mark the Coronation of Queen Elizabeth II, June, 1953.

A class at Alderman Davies Church in Wales School for Boys, Neath, 1957.

Standard 3 at St Joseph's Junior School, Port Talbot, 1956.

Pupils of Neath Boys Grammar School, with their form teacher, early 1960s.

A class at Cwmavon Junior School, 1953.

A class at Ynysmaerdy Primary School, Briton Ferry, with their teacher, Mr Thomas, 1962.

Pupils and teachers at Dyffryn Grammar School, Port Talbot, April 1960.

A class at Cwmavon Junior School with teacher and headteacher on St David's Day, 1955.

Some of the pupils at Glan Afan Grammar School, Port Talbot, November, 1953.

Pupils of Catwg Primary School, Cadoxton, Neath, in its main hall, mid-1960s.

A class at Catwg Primary School, Neath, 1967.

St David's Day 1961 saw these pupils of Central Infants School, Port Talbot, all dressed up to salute their patron saint. Behind them is their teacher.

Pupils of Park School, Port Talbot, 1963.

Some of the youngsters who attended Cylch Meithrin Skewen, 1984.

A class of pupils at Sandfields Junior School, Port Talbot, September 1959.

Children of Ambleside Nursery, George Street, Port Talbot, 1967.

The boys of the nursery class at Neath Welsh School 1985.

A class at Bryncoch Church in Wales Primary School, Neath, 1970.

Form 3 Dyffryn Comprehensive School, Margam, Port Talbot, 1967.

Children of Ambleside Nursery, George Street, Port Talbot, on St David's Day, 1967.

With lots of learning ahead of them these are some of the youngsters who attended Cylch Meithrin, Skewen, 1986.

The reception class at Alderman Davies' Church in Wales School, Neath, with their teacher Andrea Partington 1992.

Classroom activities at Groes Primary School, Bertha Road, Margam, shortly after its official opening, July 10, 1973.

St David's Day at Sandfields Infants School, 1978.

Miss Dummer's class at Blaenbaglan Primary School, Port Talbot, 1972.

Teacher Mr Redmore with class 10 at Central Junior School, Port Talbot, 1979.

Pupils at Dwr Y Felin Comprehensive School, Neath, 1999.

Industrial Insight

Kitchen staff and dinner ladies at the Gnoll School, Neath, with special guests, early 1970s.

A group of Port Talbot docks workers aboard the steam tug Emily Charlotte, early 1900s.

A corner of the Neath Sheet Steel and Galvanising Company's warehouse, 1955.

A mines rescue team in the upper Afan Valley, 1920 after a practice session.

Would-be passengers look on as some of the staff of Cymmer railway station take a break from their labours to have their picture taken, 1929.

George Davies at work in Taylor's Foundry, Briton Ferry, 1959.

A group of workmen at Port Talbot Docks, early 1940s.

Three railway platelayers at the Albion Steelworks, Briton Ferry, 1961.

BP's Llandarcy oil refinery and one of its reservoirs, August 1972.

Successful apprentices who completed their training at Baldwin's works, Port Talbot, 1947.

Workmen engaged in the making of moulds for the Albion Steelworks, Briton Ferry, at Baglan Engineering Works, Melyn, Neath, 1964.

Miners at the Hafod Colliery, Goytre, Port Talbot, early 1950s.

Nursing staff at Groeswen Hospital, Port Talbot, early 1950s.

Gnoll School dinner ladies all set to serve their hungry hordes, mid-1960s.

Aberavon window cleaner P A Reed with the hand cart he used to carry his ladder and bucket, 1962.

Colliers empty a horse-drawn dram at Goytre Colliery, Port Talbot, late 1940s.

Staff at the Colour Care photo processing laboratory, Neath Abbey, March 1, 1979.

The Metal Box factory, Neath, viewed from Evans Road, Melyncrythan, 1979.

Some of the members of the transport department of the Abbey Works, Port Talbot, 1961.

The A48 Lonlas by-pass and the EM Edwards gas works on the left, 1972.

Employees at the audiology department at Neath General Hospital enjoy some hi jinks at the farewell send off to one of their colleagues, 1993.

Landlady Seline Jones and barmaid Val Thomas of the Vivian Hotel, Victoria Road, Aberavon, pulling pints behind the bar, 1961.

Staff of Cymmer Afan Comprehensive School with headteacher Alan Benjamin, 1973.

Her Majesty Queen Elizabeth II during a tour of the Metal Box factory, Neath, during 1977, the Silver Jubilee year of her reign. Behind her are John Morris MP for Aberavon and Col Sir Cennydd Traherne, Lord Lieutenant of Glamorgan.

Full time and retained members of Glamorgan County Fire Service at Port Talbot fire station, 1974.

Part of the network of pipes that comprised the Baglan Bay complex of BP Chemicals, 1988.

Music Makers

The choir of St Theodore's Church, Port Talbot, 1936.

Pupils of the Gnoll Infants School under a garland of hand made paper lanterns during a Christmas pageant, 1953.

The Senoritas, a young jazz band formed in Margam, 1938. The girls wore black, frilly skirts and red, Spanish-style scarves. The boys were dressed as toreadors.

Participants in a concert at Eastern School, Taibach, 1950.

Some of the chorus girls of Neath Amateur Operatic Society's successful production of the Merry Widow, 1959.

A group of girls who formed part of Trixie Reed's Port Talbot dance troupe, 1948.

A scene from Cadoxton Opera Group's successful 1950 production.

Some of the performers who contributed to a successful charity fund raising event organised by Neath Evening Townswomen's Guild at the Gwyn Hall, Neath, 1966. Among them Allun Davies, one of the longest running winners on Opportunity Knocks, the popular TV talent show hosted by Hughie Green. Allun, from Neath, is pictured alongside during one of his many appearances on the show in 1965.

The choir of Cwmavon Girls' Secondary School with teacher and conductor Mr Kingsley before a performance of Handel's Messiah, 1953.

Members of the Queen Mary Stewards Jazz Band, Cwmavon, 1950s.

Some of the members of Briton Ferry Page Boys jazz band drum section after successfully taking part in a competition held at Baglan Park, Port Talbot, 1978.

The Margam Saints, a popular Port Talbot skiffle group, late 1950s. They once won a talent competition which also included Jimmy Tarbuck as a young comedian.

Members of Cadoxton Opera Group, Neath, rehearse at the town's Gnoll School for their production of the opera Nabucco at the Gwyn Hall, 1983.

Members of St David's Church Choir, Neath, 1987.

Some of those who took part in the Nativity play at St Paul's Church, Aberavon, 1962.

A band plays for passers-by in The Square, Neath, 1990.

Members of Cor Meibion, Aberavon, during a trip to Edinburgh, 1975.

Days of Religion

The chapel at Giants Grave, Briton Ferry, early 1900.

The distinctive octagonal Beulah Chapel — frequently referred to as the round chapel — at Groes, Margam, early 1900s. Nearby can be seen the village's primary school.

Members of Bethesda Chapel, Briton Ferry, during a 1950s outing.

Men and boys of the congregation of Wesley Chapel, Taibach, during a Whitsun procession 1950.

Members of the congregation of St Joseph's Roman Catholic Church, Aberavon, during a pilgrimage to Lourdes, 1950.

The cast of a Nativity play performed at St Clement's Church, Neath Road, Briton Ferry, 1952.

Children waiting to take part in a Whitsun procession at Goytre, Port Talbot, mid-1950s.

Members of Siloh Church, Melyncrythan, hold their banner high during a Whitsun march in Neath, early 1950s. Crowds line Gnoll Park Road to watch the procession.

Members of Herbert Road Baptist Church, Melyncrythan, in full voice as they head along Windsor Road, Neath, while taking part in the annual Whitsun procession, 1959.

Youngsters all set to take part in a Whitsun march at Goytre, Port Talbot, late 1950s.

The congregation and band of Skewen Salvation Army Corps, mid-1960s.

Participants in a pageant presented by members of the congregation of St Theodore's Church, Port Talbot, 1981.

Leisure and Pleasure

Shop owners and their employees from Port Talbot seen during a paddle steamer outing to Ilfracombe, North Devon, early 1920s.

A group of Neath men share a drink or two during a day out, 1939.

Officers and committee members of Taibach RFC during the club's Bournemouth tour, 1951.

A Briton Ferry family seen enjoying a camping holiday at Nottage, Porthcawl, 1949.

A Briton Ferry family enjoy a day out on the beach at Trecco Bay, Porthcawl, 1954.

Members of the congregation of Water Street English Baptist Chapel and their friends, during a trip to Blackpool, 1953.

Members of the Catholic Club, Briton Ferry Road, Melyncrythan, Neath, on an outing to Blackpool, mid-1950s.

Wives and children of employees of Port Talbot Gas Undertaking at a Christmas party held in the lower hall of Port Talbot Consitutional Club, 1953. Two male employees can be seen in the centre.

Friends and neighbours of Cove Road, Sandfields, Port Talbot, hold a party to celebrate the Coronation of Queen Elizabeth II, June, 1953.

Regulars of the Star Inn, Penydre, Neath, prepare to set off for a Scotland versus Wales rugby international at Murrayfield, mid-1950s.

Phyllis Adams hosts a tea party in the back garden of her Cove Road, Sandfields home, against a background of the prefab homes typical of the area in the early 1950s.

One of the oldest members of Skewen Salvation Army Corps is given a helping hand to cut a celebratory cake to mark a special occasion, early 1960s.

Hats and handbags all round as members of the Mother's Union at St Catwg's Church, Cadoxton, Neath, prepare for a day out, late 1950s.

Members of Bethel Chapel, Aberavon, on their 1955 Whitsun outing.

Members of Cadoxton Opera Society at the Tower Hotel, Waterford, Ireland, before their performance of Verdi's opera Nabucco at the town's prestigious annual music festival, 1965.

Staff of Woolworth's store, Station Road, Port Talbot, with its manager, Mr Williams, during their annual Christmas party, 1955.

Smartly dressed children of the Sunday school of St Paul's Church, Aberavon, enjoying their Whitsun tea, 1961.

A little girl enjoys a donkey ride at a crowded Aberavon Beach with the funfair in the background, August 1965.

Employees of the Western Welsh Bus Company's Margam Terrace, Port Talbot, depot with family and friends on their annual outing, 1962.

Family and friends at the Silver Wedding celebration of Trevor and Phyllis Jones of Cimla Crescent, Neath, 1960s.

A civic parade passes along Orchard Street, Neath, June, 1968.

A group of Port Talbot residents on a holiday break to Blackpool, 1965.

Residents and their children from Chestnut Road, Cimla, Neath, at the street party they held on Tuesday, July 1, 1969 to celebrate the Investiture of the Prince of Wales at Caernavon.

Children tuck in to the goodies on offer when residents of Bwlch Road, Cimla, Neath, held a street party to celebrate the Investiture of the Prince of Wales, July, 1969.

Women of Saltoun Street, Margam, dressed as the girls from St Trinian's during street festivities to mark the Investiture of the Prince of Wales, 1969.

These youngsters are enjoying plenty of jelly and blancmange at the second birthday party of Jason Thomas, Saltoun Street, Margam, Port Talbot, 1969.

Dancing around the Maypole, Neath style. This was the first May Day in Melyn celebration. The pole was erected in Evans Field, Melyn, 1989.

Cleaning staff from Margam Technical College, Port Talbot, enjoy a festive night out during the run up to Christmas 1973.

Members and supporters of Briton Ferry Page Boys jazz band, 1979, after winning the Welsh Open Resorts Championship at Aberavon Beach. They are pictured with the Mayor of Afan, Councillor Tom Roche, as he presents a band representative with the winners trophy.

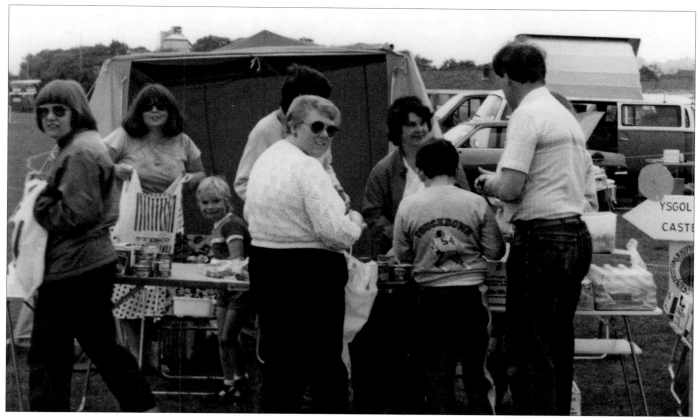

Members of the parents' association of Ysgol Gymraeg Castell Nedd — Neath Welsh Primary School — at a stall they ran at one of the town's popular annual carnivals, early 1980s.

Raising a glass at Trefelin Workingmen's Club, Velindre, Port Talbot, 1974.

Participants in the proclamation ceremony procession for the 1994 Neath and District Royal National Eisteddfod head along Gnoll Park Road towards Victoria Gardens and the Gorsedd Circle of stones. The procession took place a year before the eisteddfod, in 1993.

Parents and children of Brynglas Avenue, Cwmavon, Port Talbot, during their celebrations to mark the Silver Jubilee of Queen Elizabeth II, 1977.

The street party at Pellau Road, Margam, to celebrate the Silver Jubilee of Queen Elizabeth II, 1977.

Staff at Mor Awelon Nursing Home, Sandfields, Port Talbot, help resident Sybil Sains celebrate her birthday, 1986.

Pupils of Gnoll Primary School, Neath, on a field trip to Worm's Head, Gower, 1994.

Travel Time

The steam ship Trafalgar which ran aground at Aberavon Beach, October, 1907.

Staff and passengers at Neath Riverside station, about 1870.

The paddle steamer Cardiff Queen enters the mouth of the River Afan, Port Talbot, late 1930s.

Bus conductor Howell Phillips ready to jump aboard a South Wales Transport double decker at the company's Eastland Road depot, Neath, for his next shift, August 1959.

The Rhondda and Swansea Bay and Port Talbot Railway companies lines run alongside one another as they head up the Afan Valley near the weir at Corlannau, Port Talbot, 1920s.

A group of motorcyclists proudly show off their machines in Geoffrey Street, Neath, 1965.

Helmets didn't seem to be neccesary when motorcycle riding 1953 style at Port Talbot.

A passenger train waits at Neath Riverside Station, before heading up the Neath Valley and on to its destination, April 18, 1962.

A South Wales Transport bus company recovery crew surveys the scene after this double decker, on the No. 42 route from Swansea to Margam via Trallwn, came to grief and toppled over on the A48 at Baglan, opposite Pine Tree filling station during a wet morning in 1953.

An iron ore vessel discharges its cargo at Port Talbot docks overshadowed by blast furnaces numbers 1, 2 and 3, 1957.

Tank engine No 9484 with a train of empty coal wagons at Neath Riverside Station, April 18, 1962.

A Western Welsh bus company single decker rests between duties at the company's Margam Terrace, Port Talbot depot, mid-1950s.

Locomotive No. 5649 hauls a train of mixed freight wagons through Neath & Brecon Junction, Neath, on March 10, 1962.

Heading out of Neath Riverside station on April 13, 1962 is the 4.20pm school train, so called because it carried the town's grammar school pupils back to their Neath valley homes. Another train can be seen passing overhead in this busy scene.

Office workers pile off the buses that brought them from a variety of locations to work at Port Talbot's Abbey Works, 1952.

Buses from the fleets of Western Welsh, Thomas Bros, South Wales Transport and a variety of smaller independent operators, await the end of a shift at Port Talbot steelworks, to collect their passengers, early 1950s.

The Royal Navy cruiser HMS Bermuda at the end of her final voyage, the River Neath wharf of ship-breakers Thos. Ward at Giants Grave, Briton Ferry, 1963.

A tank engine hauls its train of freight wagons past Evans Bevan playing fields at Baglan, Port Talbot, on July 22, 1963.

A passenger train crosses the River Neath on May 31, 1963.

A mixed freight train, including oil wagons, heads east through Port Talbot General Station, on July 31, 1963.

With Margam Terrace clearly visible in the background, locomotive 7215 heads a train of wagons through Port Talbot General Station, on July 4, 1963.

Locomotive No. 82000 tops up its tanks from the water pump at the end of one of the platforms at Neath General railway station on December 28, 1963.

A train heads west through Port Talbot railway station, on August 8, 1964.

Pannier tank locomotive No 4639 hauls a passenger train over the River Neath on September 21, 1963 after leaving Neath General railway station.

A passenger train heads through Neath Junction, May 27, 1963.

A Treherbert to Neath passenger train hauled by locomotive No 6641 leaves Aberavon Town Station on June 11, 1964, crossing the roadway at High Street and no doubt causing traffic tailbacks in the process.

Milkman Ron Llewellyn who worked on many rounds in both Neath and Port Talbot at the wheel of his electric milk float in New Henry Street, Neath, mid-1960s.

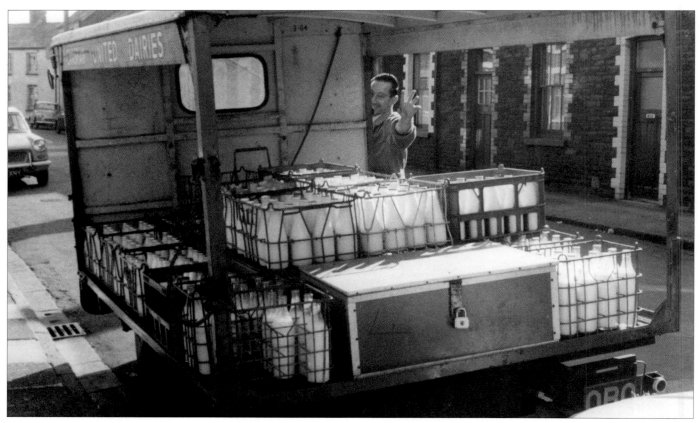

Milkman Ron Llewellyn with his loaded Cambrian United Dairies milk float during an early morning delivery at New Henry Street, Neath, 1964.

Two different views of station buildings at the town terminus of the former Port Talbot Railway, 1967. They stood between Eagle House and the Plaza Cinema until they were demolished in 1969.

A meeting of motive power. Steam and diesel are both in evidence in this busy scene at Neath General Station, 1964.

A Thomas Bros Leyland Tiger Cub bus at Efail Fach, September 13, 1967. It was heading back to Port Talbot from Tonmawr at the time.

A trio of Western Welsh Leyland vehicles on the forecourt of Neath railway station, 1965.

Buses lined up in the forecourt of Neath General station, early 1920s. The vehicle at the front is a Great Western Railway bus used on a connecting service to Pontardawe.

A Thomas Bros Leyland Tiger bus waits in Bethany Square, Port Talbot, April 4, 1968.

This Western Welsh bus had been involved in a road accident at Crynant, 1964.

A steam tug heads out of the mouth of the River Afan, 1960.

Early construction work underway on the right, for the Llandarcy to Aberdulais section of the A465 trunk road dual carriageway, 1972.

Locomotive No 3634 at Glynneath, February 6, 1964. The two carriage, local train is heading down the valley for Neath.

A Llynfi Motors bus passes Chapel of Ease, Port Talbot, on its way into the town with passengers from Bryn, July 1987.

A line up of fishing and pleasure craft near the mouth of the River Afan, Port Talbot, April 1988.

Game Players

This was the Neath RFC team which played Pontypridd on March 6, 1936.

Pony and trap drivers line up to decide the best turned out entrant in a competition held at Port Talbot, early 1900s. The venue later became the Talbot Athletic Ground. Houses in Penycae can be seen in the background.

Players tackle the 9th hole at Neath
Golf Club, 1936.

Aberavon boxers
Edwin Jones, left;
Mog Pugh, centre
and Joe Hopkins,
1936.

Players and officials of Taibach
RFC, Port Talbot, 1890.

Members of the rugby squad at Central Junior School, Port Talbot, 1935-36.

Penrhiwtyn Youth Club, Neath, first and second Sunday afternoon football teams 1947.

One of the rugby squads at Trefelin Secondary School, Port Talbot, 1950s.

Neath and District Schools' football team, at Cwrt Sart School playing fields, 1966.

Neath Boys' Grammar School football squad with their teacher, 1972.

Glan Afan Grammar School under 15 rugby team, 1952-53.

Players and officials of Taibach RFC, Port Talbot, 1950-51.

Members of the successful FC Nedd football team fielded by Neath Boys Club who were Neath League Division Three champions and cup winners in the 1976-77 season.

The cricket XI at Dyffryn Grammar School, Port Talbot, with headteacher and teachers, 1954.

Cwmavon School rugby team, 1956-57 season with the school's sports master and headteacher.

Members of the Gnoll Junior School, Neath, soccer team, proudly display their mascots and the spoils of a successful days play, May 1978. With them are the team reserves and teachers.

Baglan United under 18s soccer team 1955-56 season.

Members of Neath Boys Club's successful FC Nedd football team behind an impressive line-up of trophies and awards at their 1979-80 season presentation evening.

Young members of Neath Athletic RFC getting some last minute tactical tips from Wyndham Griffiths, one of their coaches, during their 1994 French tour.

Glan Afan Grammar School senior cricket team, mid-1950s.

Port Talbot YMCA under 18s soccer team 1963-64 who were undefeated that season.

Members of the Aberavon Green Stars rugby team which toured Kilkenny in Ireland, Easter 1963.

Baglan Cricket Club players and officials — plus their young mascot — 1972.

Pupils of Dyffryn Comprehensive School, Port Talbot, sailing on Eglwys Nunydd reservoir, Margam, mid-1970s. The British Steel Corporation's plant is silhouetted in the background.

Members of Neath Athletic's under 14 team during their successful tour to France, 1994.

Baglan RFC under 10 rugby team which emerged as runners up in an all Wales final for their age group at Cardiff Arms Park, late 1970s after beating off competition from more than 200 teams.

A rugby team consisting of parents and teachers at Neath Welsh School with members of a team from popular Welsh TV soap opera Pobl Y Cwm, 1990s.

Youngsters from Tonna AFC, Neath, with soccer star Ryan Giggs before taking up their duties as ball boys at a Welsh International at Cardiff Arms Park, mid-1990s.

Presentation of awards by Lord Heycock in the presence of other local dignitaries to pupils of Dyffryn Comprehensive School, Port Talbot, who represented Wales at varying levels of different sports during 1981.

The British Steel Corporation's Port Talbot works cricket team, 1983.

The netball team at Glan Afan Comprehensive School, Port Talbot, with the school's gym teacher and headteacher 1987.